Collision With the Shadow

Also by Carolyn Gerrish
The Ground Slides Away (Five Islands Press)
Learning to Breathe Under Water (Island Press)
Hijacked to the Underworld (Five Islands Press)
Dark Laughter (Island Press)
The View from the Moon (Five Islands Press)

Carolyn Gerrish

Collision With the Shadow

Acknowledgements

Some of the poems in this collection have appeared
in the following publications:
Australian Poetry Journal, *Best Australian Poems*, *The Burrow*,
The Canberra Times, *Famous Reporter*, Central Coast Poets
Anthology: *The Way to the Well*, Don Bank Live Poets Anthology
2011, *foam:e*, *Mascara Literary Review*, *Notes for the Translators
Anthology*, *Poets at the Pub Anthology* 2013, *Rampike*, *Shot Glass
Journal*, Spineless Wonders Journal: *Not Very Quiet*, Australian
Speculative Poetry: *The Stars Like Sand*, Young Street Poets
anthologies: T*his Strange World*, *Naming the Particulars*.

My special thanks to John Carey for invaluable editorial assistance.
My gratitude to Brenda Saunders for the cover graphic and layout.
Thanks also to Young Street Poets and Round Table Poets
for their ongoing support.

Collision With the Shadow
ISBN 978 1 76109 240 4
Copyright © text Carolyn Gerrish 2022
Cover image: Brenda Saunders
Stock Photos USA

First published 2022 by
Ginninderra Press
PO Box 3461 Port Adelaide 5015
www.ginninderrapress.com.au

Contents

Dark Matter
    Hauntings   11
    Doppelganger   12
    War of Nerves   13
    Nemesis   14
    Domestic Apparitions   15
    Chamber of Horrors   16
    Zombies   17
    FX   19
    Dark Matter   20
    Apocalypse   21
    Parallel Universe   22
    Confronting the Monster   23
    Fiend Redeemed   25
    Edgy   26
    Creepy Vibes   27
    Sleepless in Sydney   29

Culture Club
    The 'Ring Thing'   33
    Comments on an Opera by Verdi   34
    Performance Pieces   35
    After Hearing Enescu's String Octet, Opus 7   38
    Bette Davis Eyes   39
    Lines after Film Stars Don't Die in Liverpool   40
    Bill Henson Narrative   41
    Riffing on Louise Hearman   42
    Ground Zero   43
    Triptych   44
    Chill-out Room   46
    All My Own Work   47

Litbits	48
Tattoo Gallery	50
Absurdity Rules	51
Familiarity	52
Litbits 2	53
Surreal	54
Aperture	55

In Treatment

Holding Pattern	59
Scars	60
WWER	61
In Treatment	63
Obsessive Compulsive	64
An injured umbrella	66
Prosthetic	67
Cataracts	69
Specialist	70
because of a possible overdose	71
Recovery	72
Mental Hospital Movie	73
Recipe for Weariness	75
Side Effects	76
Bad Medicine	77

Close to Home

Solastalgia	81
Disconnect	83
Impact	84
Flying Footwear	86
Ventilation	87
The Life of Rooms	88
Domestic	89

Exercise Class	91
Café Society	92
Lost Property Office	93
Lunchtime Meditation	94
The Bells	96
Atmospherics	98
Inner City Blues	99
Phone Home	100
From the Park Bench	101
Nature Lines	102
Footpath Theatre	104
Figures in the Landscape	106
Treelined	107
In Transit	108
Sky Poems	109
Reprise	111

From a Foreign Country

Memoir	115
Genealogy	117
A Disappointed Life	120
Window	122
Glimpse	124
Identity	125
Sprung	126
Pedestrians	127
Signpost	128

Dark Matter

One does not need to be a chamber to be haunted
– Emily Dickinson

Hauntings

they come calling   pawing at doors &
windows   *let me in   i'm so cold*   their
hoarse voices   mist from floorboards
ceilings & hallways   how to persuade a ghost
to move on   get a life   (exorcisms   so messy)
but they have a stake in shadowy perpetuation
& any lack of focus   from the living   can
encourage a bogeyman   they're omnipresent
invisible at corporate meetings   hiding in the
powerpoint   able to alter the flexible past
& there   in the windless garden   a child's
swing   creaking back & forth & a cadaver
emerges from the unlit café   phantom limb
kicks an empty crisps packet   onto the
noir street

& perhaps you need the shining   to apprehend
something so varied & wandering   that spectral
diaspora   unable to rest   you appear to be
human   but are quickly cut dead   by a friend
who walks away   waving to the anonymous air
& a clairvoyant shuffles/cuts cards   claims
intimacy with the underworld   *someone who has
passed over   is with you   today*

Doppelganger

1

to forget yourself   put concerns on hold
you go to look at pictures   but you're
still there   ghosting in the frame   your
head   attached to clouds   superimposed
over a skeletal arm   immanent in yellow
smoke   immersed in the chiaroscuro &
wonder if these created images   have more
reality than **you**   so the seduction of other
vicarious worlds   is denied
>   *for the other*
>   *who haunts me*
>   *& whom I haunt*

II

facing the slim ebony screen
entertainment inactive
your double   a headless body
a revenant in the living room
identity at a distance
curtains   obscure outside's
anaemic light   glide open
reveal an aperture   where an
ectoplasmic figure   resides

War of Nerves

sometimes   the feeling nothing can harm you
the dizziness of freedom   where anxiety's
a useless passion & there's no vigil waiting
for the end to begin   you've lost the fear
life could just haemorrhage away   or that the
mobile phone tower   could morph into a Transformer
& ruin the suburb & there's plucky Bette Davis
who   after receiving a negative prognosis   from
the handsome doctor   claims   *I'm young & strong &*
nothing can touch me
       every exit
              is an entry
                      somewhere else

but why are there so many security guards at the
Mall   then there's the worry of wrong weather
(this year   summer was autumn) & those nimbus clouds
painters' inspiration   or evidence of Apocalypse
& that shadow   just resting on the road   becomes a
suspected portent & please note   the asteroid
passing by us   if we collide   *could certainly*
take out a medium-sized continent   so   with
Armageddon averted for now   one antagonist
is missing   but the 24 hour news cycle never
stops   as a rogue Afghan soldier   kills
Australian troops
       the disaster
              takes care
                      of everything

Nemesis

everything belonging to my goth neighbour
is black   including her cat   it likes to sit
in queenly territoriality on the fire stairs
observing the world from a great height   or
engaging in agitated ablutions   if i approach
i'm greeted with a snarl   or yowl   once wrongly
attempting to make feline-face-contact
was rewarded with a wounding scratch down
the arm   have i been cursed with a satanic spell
engineered by my ritualistic neighbour   who
insists her ferocious pet is 'just scared'
sometimes it does retreat   tail headed towards
the cat door   trailing like a doleful fashion accessory
& being no longer athletic   makes an ungainly
leap through the kitchen window – a shameful
inconvenient act

yesterday   sitting at the ground floor window
was a beautiful grey moggie   who stared out
at the world with a sense of tranquillity   we
can't always choose who lives near us

Domestic Apparitions

even if you can't believe it
this house is infested with ghosts
there's the face of Arthur Stace
on the bubble-glass door &
invisible feet   make the floorboards
creak   look   a stoic backbone of light on
the lounge room wall & a transparent
child stares rapt in a rock   the presence
of pain sits patient in this room & *i must
flee what is darkest in me*

   & outside   propped
   against the brick wall
   an extension ladder
   of shadow available
   for those without bodies

& near the window arms crossed &
power dressed is a revenant female
manager   she points to a filing cabinet
where names of past residents are kept
she sees me as imminently absent – *you
are not meant to be   here when will
you leave* – (but I'm certainly not going to
move) then was it her or me or something
else that said
> *remember we're still here*
>   *after we've gone*

'i must flee what is darkest in me' – from 'Age Appropriate', Phillip Schultz

Chamber of Horrors

always a sinister streak   a fixation on dark things
the dolorous tolling of bells & a coven of crows
in the camphor laurel & this weird desire to tell
narratives of necrophilia in saturated colours
instead   a flock of black zeros follow you
they're coming to get you Barbara   but those
stalking noughts   really add to your day
especially when they opine – why settle for
something   when you can have nothing –
then you arrive home & an intuition strikes
you need extraterrestrials about you   not this
replicant   staring at your red shoes & what
you wouldn't give   for a rave with Gollum
or a goblin or a zombie   you could inquire
if they were preparing for an interview with
the vampire & you they will reply that
yes there will be blood   but first they would
like to haunt the garden of their eternal
past   to revisit their venus flytraps

Zombies

They're everywhere. On the move. Shuffling
unwholesomely. Could never pass as refugees.
(Being homeless never bothered them). Yet no
one is free of them. Even Jane Austin is implicated.
Mr Darcy gets to fight them.

Zombies are an existential paradox in the thrilling
hiatus between life and death. In Australia, some
climbed out of their graves in a mogadon haze.
Yet scrubbed up well after a bath. Others, photogenic
as movie stars, were found as a flash mob somewhere
in the French Alps. Street cred urban zombies conduct
languid rallies:

> *What do we want?*
>   *A tasty brain*
> *When do we want it?*
>   *No need to rush*

Am I tempted to join them? No fear. I'm not sufficiently
deceased.
  And I will not negotiate with the un-dead.

Sometimes, though, it's difficult to establish
who's actually dead and who's still among the living.

I'd prefer to be composing a poem than exploring aspects
of subhuman decomposition.
  Shake not thy gory locks at me

Perhaps my affinity for fantasy has abandoned me.
I fail to see why zombies are considered cool. Is it
because they're so gruesomely independent? Rejecting
conventional career paths? Refusing to multi-skill?
Being repulsive, is after all a full-time vocation.
Just hanging out, is enough.

FX

if you aspire to high-definition splendour
without first having experienced your own labyrinth
it could be a tragic endgame   your empathetic self
co-opted by space invaders   thanks to the magic of
CGI & there'll be no more stalking Solaris
to see which one of you is real   but remember you'll
never be alone   while you sup with clones
existence as it is   without meaning or aim

& this desire for something bigger (& noisier)
than ourselves   welcome *Rosemary's Baby* & *Carrie*
bringing   ultraviolence & telekinetic outcomes to
die for   but not funambulist Phillipe Petit who
hiked across heaven for 45 minutes (such *ecstatic*
nihilism) without the need to photoshop   or
Felix Baumgartner   freefalling to earth   & look
mum   no teleportation   *everything becomes &*
recurs eternally

at this stage of the game   there could be gunplay
but more likely the *cruel miracle* of drone-controlled
extinction & the right to erase oneself becomes more
than a possibility   *but you've got to be alive to*
be scared   though **ABANDON HOPE** is scrawled over
an animatronic sky & out there   believe it or not
Ripley   *thought in its most terrible form happens*
& there are no cockroaches left for the cat to eat
in space   no one can hear you dream   or mouth the
mantra **RULE DYSTOPIA**

Dark Matter

staring into the void
at twenty
someone may catch you
if you fall –
staring into the void
at sixty-five –
just a black hole

*

window on the night
Rothko bleakness

*

they all want a piece of me
(she said)   but the last morsel
was swallowed long ago

*

the never-opened bookcase
glass doors   reflect window bars

*

how heartening to see
finally   a haikuist
makes the obituaries

Apocalypse

without asking permission
the sun goes for a dip
as do the clouds & the sky
revelling in the cosmic soup
leaving everything to gape
a cupboard revealing secrets
but don't open your eyes
or you'll notice all that's left
of the world   is an averted face
its heart   no longer in residence
(& the sleeve cruelly ripped
where it sometimes lay bare)
you finally find a place to rest
while waiting for the end)
the roof   everlasting in its rustiness
inside though   you can dream
in the chiaroscuro room
where the winding sheets whisper
'go & close the windows'

Parallel Universe

At 3 p.m.
the marble fireplace   prefers to
walk off   across the wet grass
even onto the powdery snow &
the pictures on the wall have gone
returned to their dodgy provenance
& that climbing plant silhouette
frissons across the window frame
only original instruments may play
& the death of Schubert begins again
quick   pull the blinds for a private
hearing   then we can all leave &
not wait for the chandelier to fall

we've excavated   discovered the bones
of the matter   found a habitation
where no fiend can fit   then   celebrating
we'll go down to the sea   where there's
no need for explanations & a woman
walks calmly   deep along the bottom

Confronting the Monster

was it you who let the Thing inside?
face hugger   chest buster a bit squishy &
gnarled   more earthy than the weeping angels
rejecting all taxonomic rules   quite unlovely
really   no need to search for aliens at the outer-
limits   this monster   your freaky doppelganger
lives here   intimates together in the womb (though
it had many lives before)   the creature births first
hell-bent into the open room   its choice to be
invisible (or not)   alive on earth   yet *cut off from
all the world*

you're used to its unsociable habits   the way it wants
to devour everyone (except you) & a penchant for
destroying new apartment blocks   not to mention
its conflagratory breath   yet how perversely cool to
bond with a nightmare & channelling your inner-
godzilla   gives a boost to self-esteem & promenading
with a ghastly handbag (an awesome buddy) keeps
harassers at bay

but ultimately   its monsterdom overwhelms   that
basilisk stare   erodes your motivation   you feel like
lying down among the dead   wondering if you should
still be here & difficult to ignore those marauding threats
misery made me a fiend and *i shall cause fear*   if it
were less colossal you could lock it away   just
something nasty in the woodshed

your rejection of misshapen otherness wins out &
defriending a monster is easy   you just say – it isn't
working – & immediately you're alien-free   your
frightening 'friend' departs   boards a mothership
goes into hypersleep   *what slumbers there   is not
human*   then   a voyage of interstellar infinity through
wormholes   disembarks on an unknown planet?
leaving you standing alone on terra firma   doomed
to the pathos of normality

'cut off from all the world/misery made me a fiend/I shall cause fear'
– from *Frankenstein*, Mary Shelley

Fiend Redeemed

your Inner Monster   is tired of you
wants a change of scene   a full-time
freaking-out vocation   is too onerous
always having to ensure there is a sense
of crisis & anxiety   they move out into
the community   lose their horror status –
but sometimes   memories of their dark
apprenticeship   begin to overwhelm
& they paint black apocalyptic clouds
all over the bus timetables

Edgy

though seeming to belong   the interloper
always positioned at the back of the room
spaceship parked outside   ready for speedy
leave-taking   or   hovering above the
inner circle   completing an aerial shot (for
proof of who was there) later when
questioned by authorities   without needing
an autocue she says – I only come for the
teacake – the interloper (a dissembler)
can suss out another gate-crasher
one of the living dead   in a black dress &
shawl   pretending to enact some anachronistic
tragedy   the interloper   always searching
beyond the banal   where to find the archetypal
mind?   she'd seen it once but lost it   while
climbing a style   looking for the lost words
of Wordsworth   yes
> *the world is*
>
> > *too much with us*

the interloper   (often austere as a Carl Dreyer
film)   is quick to reject the saccharine verdict
after the serenade was played & the applause
– lovely   very nice – the interloper knows
there's no wisdom found at the Convenience Store
she's **there** yet not always **present** & can see
through the person on the empty chair   knows
the outcome before the end   transcending
autobiography
> *like a ghost*
>
> > *forever in the world*

26

Creepy Vibes

a young woman
boards the bus
turns into a witch
flies off at the next stop

*

the hedge near the fence
shivers in the evening breeze

*

fruit bats   arrive
populate the camphor laurel
their strangled baby cries
& velvet flapping –
so spooky

*

further down the road
a dead bat   hangs
on the power line –
a ragged black bag

*

Halloween was last week
but she still wears
skulls on her t-shirt
she dreams a man
with an unpleasant message
is waiting outside

*

the door to the kitchen
opens by itself –
hungry ghost

               *

at 3 a.m. –
that strange pale hour
of morning –
an illuminated truck
with no driver
speeds through the darkness

Sleepless in Sydney

you know there's something wrong
with the moon   that *pale-night
wanderer*   has it come adrift &
headed for your room?   afraid if
you stared too long outside   the
sky would disappear

   the geology
        of worry
                   how it burrows
                            into the morning

just a two-note call of an early
mournful bird & someone scurries
to the street   with a forgotten bin

the old desk fan   asthmatic in the
dark & why this riot in the chest
(neighbour's aircon   or just you?)
oh   if only I had someone else's heart
i know I would never fall apart   could
return to the time before everything
was broken   go away   go away   the tune
in my head   not mine instead it's my
mother's Barcarole   now it's all very
clear   there's never a way out of here
can you retrieve your resilience?   stolen
by the wind   suspended somewhere
distant   like discarded washing

Culture Club

Art is what you can get away with
– Andy Warhol

If you don't know the exact moment
when the lights go out, you might as well read
– Clive James

The 'Ring Thing'

on the wettest day for thirty years   *what wild tale*
is this   leaving the theatre   not wanting to come down
full of sorrow & dread   lost in the leitmotifs that
encore   take residence in the mind   *did I dream such*
rapture & such a crowdpleaser when Valhalla (that
mcmansion in the clouds) incinerates   all your fault
Wotan   hiding behind your eyepatch   shouldn't have
slept around (particularly with humans)   **will you**
stop rustling that bag   will you stop crunching
those nuts   & Brunnhilde   even with your helmet
breastplate & sassiness   all over for you when you
fell for Siegfried   a bloke who knew no fear & found
death such a breeze   no need for palliative care
its terrors are blissful

   & you see Brunnhilde's face over the
   IGA sign   Wotan's walking stick now
   belongs to a pedestrian & those police
   sirens shrilling down Oxford Street
   really Rhine Maidens fending off a
   randy Dwarf & Comancheros scaring
   the traffic   beware the Valkyries
   will soon overtake you   then the
   ring slips from your finger   falls
   into a grate on the footpath

Comments on an Opera by Verdi

Be warned, for those with aural sensitivities, (particularly those with tinnitus). The music is extremely loud. Particularly the ear-splitting chorus at the end of Act 3. Also unnerving are the gunshots blasting throughout the performance. And, unfortunately, for digital phobics, tweets are actively encouraging during the interval, dispelling all histrionic illusion.

For those queasy about transvestites, there's a male actor wearing a frock. And if you have a low tolerance to ballet, there's a nauseating abundance of it here, including a surfeit of fairy wings.

This production has a distinctly funereal tone, so may not suit audience members with melancholic tendencies. Many of the cast wear skull masks and an executioner's block is centre stage. And there are some confronting inconsistencies regarding the purported age of the protagonists. Anyone with half an eye could see that the tenor who plays the son is the same age as the baritone playing his father.

Also, the character played by the soprano (in spite of looking gorgeous and singing like an angel), suffers from cognitive dissonance. She believes that a half-naked child, wielding a cardboard scythe, has the power to behead her. And the romantic tenor, alas, is bursting out of his vest and breeches from the merciless pastas of a doting nonna.

Performance Pieces

Curtain Calls

after the end   they stay
not wanting to leave &
hoping for some encore or
another act   that would
delay the fact of a return
to reality with its certainty
of annoyance & worry   the
chorus   advance still in
their prison clothes & the
love-obsessed woman who
drowned herself & her rival
in a lake   is a fake   she's here
dry & fully resuscitated   as she
waves to her besotted audience
with all the playfulness of
a coquette

The Reject Poem

life's too short —
can't pretend when attending a group
causing endless yawning
abscond   flee to your own remoteness
& you refuse to stay at a play
where the female protagonist
is a natural narcissist
even though the critics say
the actor gave a *powerhouse performance*
you would have loved to pull the plug
on such unenlightened elocution
sometimes the jagged pulse
of the jackhammer outside
is preferable
& when a friend talks of *someone's sin*
It's hard not to tell them
to bin that thought
such a medieval idea
though Dante's hell
has a certain allegorical frisson
      thinking by death
               to escape the world's distain

Ambivalence

i wanted to disappear
or   did I really want
to stand up tall   to
make them hear what
i said   a quickening
rant   before we all
were dead

After Hearing Enescu's String Octet, Opus 7

you've such a need for harmony
can't be mesmerised by acoustic
misery   the biting insects of those
shrieking scratchy strings   you need
to slap at   or duck & hide from –
all shout at once   everyone wants
to be heard   this agony of life   yet
still with energy to suffer on
suddenly   the quarrelling stops
dissonance becomes distance
without an echo

Bette Davis Eyes

i know I've said this before but I don't dream much anymore then again   I don't sleep much either   gone are those night flights to elsewhere when a dream lands near me   i wind it tightly around me   so it doesn't float away into the amnesia of early morning

*

i'm in the back seat of a car with my friend   Bette Davis is at the wheel   she negotiates the traffic with sassy bravura   we pass parks   posh harbour suburbs outlying places car graveyards docklands   warehouses that invite gangland shootouts

*

she's my favourite screen star I want to impress her   try reciting some of her best lines   capture her sense of wounded incredulity *'What a dump'*   her shoulders twitch   she gives a soft cackle i could never compete with her delicious schadenfreude but continue *'Eve Eve Little Miss Evil'* she nods I'm really revved up now *'Fasten your seatbelts It's sure to be a bumpy night'* the car shudders   stops   she turns   those famous eyes spit venom at me '**Going to be** *a bumpy night   most certainly not* **sure to be**'

*

there's a histrionic silence   with a wounding jolt the car moves we descend a precariously steep hill   i had no idea Bette was such a pedant   but she was right I was wrong   I wanted to apologise   my friend touches my arm   *'Let her concentrate on the driving she can't tolerate anything that alters the perfection of her greatest performance'*

Lines after *Film Stars Don't Die in Liverpool*

at the end   no romance remained
just grief   washed out into the rainy
streets   only shadows   infest the room
where she confronts her mirror   plays
song for guy on a tinny cassette player
she won't say die – *i can get better i
know i can* – did she take those pills
on the table   perhaps more important
were the lipstick & mascara – *how do
i look?* – actresses were meant to play
tragic heroines   but would always survive
their deaths   for drinks in the green room

not long ago   she slammed the surgery door
no film offers   instead walked the boards
time not wasted   all too quickly gone
that door with hope for a cure   now locked –
downstairs   her young lover worries   but
that won't save her   his *drop of anguish*
will dissolve   soon he'll forget his famous
movie star   taste a new life

Bill Henson Narrative

After Bill Henson *Cloud Landscapes* photography exhibition – Art Gallery of NSW 2013

she's incognito   lying in a cave   hair
over her face   that's the way she wants it
the only way to be free   is lock yourself
away   the outside doesn't exist   the
scenery isn't seen   a reedy swamp   ragged
apron of water   a forest   possessing a
threatening fairy tale she'd already
inhabited   but she **would** accept a ride
on a mattress of cloud   voyaging
elsewhere   dissolving bodies populate
her dreams & in a chalky red sky   a cypress
agitates   like a fiery pagoda
                                        in the past
she's dressed   for the trance   knowing her
clothes   would soon fall from her & she
joined the boy   who'd been watching her &
they kissed   then   he bent back   so thin
yet he doesn't break & he upends his
wine bottle   so as not to miss the dregs
of a life   too short to lose & in the
distance   at the end of the road   a
numinous space   awaits

Riffing on Louise Hearman

After Louise Hearman Exhibition, Museum of Contemporary Art, Sydney 2016

There's nothing normal in these atmospheres. Such surfaces
of disquiet. An otherworldly light over a cathedral of trees.
A glow from nowhere. The presence of the numinous?
See that cloud, like a punching bag. Who would have thought
the air had such attitude. Has someone hallucinated
a snub-nosed child into this landscape with no content?
On the ground those solid yellow shapes. Rocks? Sandbags?
Diseased teeth after a lifetime of smoking? But you could trudge
for miles along the road. Cry out in alarm when it disappears.

Yet there are **more** children far from schools' unwelcome discipline. But their punishment for absenteeism is disembodiment. Head and shoulders of a boy/girl in a Prussian blue swamp. Others with no legs to flee from harm. A young woman meditates   as a slimy extraterrestrial glides up to greet her. Will she take the bait and mate with lizardly otherness? Look, a large empathic dog sits on the aurora borealis. Who says there's no afterlife for animals? The weather, though, can turn scary. Pull the ears off a cat. A predator bird takes centre stage. Poses against the settling sun. Will these tremors we experience disappear if we ever wake up.

Ground Zero

After Rita Lazauskas, *View from the Ramparts # 5* mixed media drawing

the omniscient narrator peers down   the air
stoic rather than heroic   no *ignorant armies*
(that) *clash by night*   & Stendahl would find
nothing to swoon about   it's just a mess of stuff
detritus of the city's zeitgeist & are these
your pets? dogs? camels? a baby in a backpack
on the way to Kindergarten Adventure Travel   &
objects Jung would love to discuss   a key for
no particular door   residences are generic here
a torch to search for your neglected self   a
globe of the world beginning to shatter after
ignoring all the warnings   a lady's hat housing
no skull & sheep & goats wander the street & *he
shall set the sheep on his right hand   but the
goats on the left*   a decaying apple   brain in
cognitive decline *when I am dead & doctors know
not why*   a life-size doll with attitude & paint
brushes that achieve an extinguished palette
but unfolding   unfolding   *as being emerges
from concealment*

Triptych

Nun's Eye View

Sister Wendy bespectacled lisping through
buck-teeth gauchely ethereal in antiquated
habit conducts viewers through the world's
art museums for years lived like a gypsy
in a caravan reading art history confesses
i wanted passionately to love God exchanges
prayer-life for delight in the *glorious male
nude* (Saint Sebastian Caravaggio's youths)
with all the frisson of the celibate & expounds
tender biographies Giorgione died young
Watteau had TB Klee scleroderma *Botticelli
knew what it was like to be alone* unlike Wendy
who always had a personal saviour to draw on

Pre-Raphaelite Quickie

attendant in black he's legally loitering
not part of the art seen it all before as
cultural consumers crawl along the wall delight
in familiar art candy **she's** wearing a furry
mauve scarf tells her husband – 'of course I'm
always studying' – pauses in front of *Mariana*
(eyes closed tragically hands pressed against back
in need of a chiropractor?) then rushes forward
to a beautiful corpse (not looking at all dead
tastefully decked out in pink flowers crows at
a respectful distance) – come on – she says
– we need to hurry so much to get through
before the luncheon –

Picasso Overkill

– we're going on a journey – she says to
her daughter at the entrance   smorgasbord
of misshapen women   one   a giant slug
for a nose   another like an elephant   a
third   deformed arms (thalidomide victim?)
& here's one   head split down the middle
(much too late for medical intervention)
– it's great fun isn't it? – & away from
the carnage   the arts commentator sits
serenely applying her lipgloss

Chill-out Room

After Pipilotti Rist *Mercy Garden Retour Skin*, six-channel video installation, sound, carpet, pillows,19th Biennale of Sydney 2014

from out of the storm they come. sink to the floor.
nothing to fear. three walls of ocean rise above.
yet no one drowns. yellow rose in a red sea. a tongue
probes beneath the water. then a shifting forest.
rorschach. opens out. a boy runs to a wall. to merge
with a fugitive cosmos. welcome to the life immersive.
enter here and leave all analytical thought behind. as
pleasure is the only thing to live for. only whispering
is encouraged. even for those watchers along the back
wall. tattoo of shadow flowers. pink rose bobbing in
water. & seagulls everywhere. guitar riffs & *i never
dreamed i'd meet somebody like you.* edenic. hedonic.
was arcadia ever lost? supine friends on facebook.
phone-photos-incandescence. but this experience has
to be lived. old couples on the floor, find it hard to rise.
but after this. how can anyone face the rain outside?

All My Own Work

After Nigel Milsom, *Judo House Part 6. The White Bird*, 2015
Archibald Prize, Art Gallery of NSW

the need-to-read wall caption
never mentions Bernini   or that
tourist-riddled sculpture a
swooning spiritual moment –
Saint Theresa   levitating in her
gravity-defying marble drapery
close by   a motivated angel
spear-poised   to give her a dose
of God   *all the senses are taken*
up with this joy   **he's** burgled
her ecstasy & her image   (original
depictions of modern passion just
don't do it)   against a dark ground
he's **painted** her   in white & blue/grey
(no attribution to the past master)
but he would probably say   he was
impressed by its Baroque histrionics
&   the wonderful potential for contrast
but the vision (of course) was his alone

Litbits

Overwhelmed

enter bookshop
with gift voucher
the luxury of choice –
smorgasbord of pages
too many to taste

Then

It was my summer
of phoney haiku –
a real poet
needs to find lines
for no particular reason
whatever the season –
did Plato ever
stopping thinking   to
enjoy a gelato
or a Greek salad

Your Muse

is currently unavailable
please wait until pages
become responsive

Gone Books

to the person who stole
my green-striped shopping bag
while I was reading
in the food court
I **do** hope you're enjoying
the Alice Munro short stories
plus the more esoteric pleasures
from the latest *Australian
Poetry Journal*   it would be
a great pity if you happened
to be culturally illiterate

Tattoo Gallery

why go under the needle?   a dare   after an inebriated night? *Warning: Contents Under Pressure*   or a message of true love *Kerry Forever*   (when she's no longer there) or maybe not just a narcissistic need to be seen   but an enjoyment in the emerging narrative   the sense that the skin is a wasted *tabula rasa*   *My Body is My Journal* & what of the woman who shaved her head to display a portrait of her cat   now in a perfect position to catch birds
  wear your heart
       on your skin

where do our tattoos go after we die? it seems that we can bequeath them to family or gift them to friends but such unique artistry   is not just skin deep   deserves a more mystical afterlife   consider a possible Tattoo Eschatology   images of angels   babies   love hearts Jesus & peace signs   would go to the Blessed Land for Inked Skin   but skull & crossbones   serpents   devils birds of prey & misogynistic graphics   are destined for the Other Place

very soon a nerdy start-up   will buy & exhibit tattoos from the deceased   collectors' items   sold to the highest bidder (after consultation with the funeral home & authorised flaying)
     the palest ink
          will outlast
               the memory of men

Absurdity Rules

sometimes   being cheerful isn't easy
that ability to smile at someone else's child
throwing a public tantrum & having the discipline
not to abuse the bus driver when he's
forty minutes late & trying not to flinch
when someone says of a recently deceased relative
'I wonder what wonderful adventures she's having'
no   your default position is a *sweet dour pessimism*
where the soundtrack of your days is a Brahms
string sextet   but you can bring out the hilarity
in bleakness   like the Hanged Man   turn everything
on its head   so even the worst calamity can be
laughed at
   my way of laughing
      is to tell the truth

so the only **real** catastrophe occurs when your pen
runs out   while trying to record a *Chaser Moment*
& those *belle époque* Rupert Bunny women clutching
fans & roses & staring existentially into the night
could they be waiting for a take-away pizza?   then
while the lights are off   an auteur projects a
fictional film of your life-in-progress but
the plot is vertiginous   the colour palette
confusing (even rainbows have doppelgangers)
the protagonist is unlikeable & it's no joke when
she misplaces her sanity   then discovers her soulmate
is a paedophile serial killer
   comedy is a tragedy
      with a happy ending

Familiarity

make the music stop   the tune is unfamiliar
& why have those Schumann etudes deserted me
& given the choice i would always prefer the
accustomed knife-thrusts of Bernard Herrmann
to some anodyne soundtrack & the climax of
Vertigo   always reassuringly distressing
watching Kim Novak die   again   as she falls
from the bell tower & there's the happiness
of recognition   when you meander through rooms
of paintings   rediscover *The Peaceable Kingdom*
naïve piles of quiescent animals staring ahead
at the viewer & the sense of déjà vu
that i might have lived in that desolate grey
Edward Hopper house on that uncanny quiet
street

> *to wander about in times*
>   *that do not belong to us*

& finally   to return to the predictable
assuagement of home   what a revelation
to surprise a recognised intruder   who's
usurping your bedroom   just your own
reflection in the cheval mirror

> *for what is life*
>   *for me*
>   *without thee*

Litbits 2

Competition Judge

my shortlist
is suffering long-life fatigue

On Not Winning Literary Competitions

sometimes you're
a bridesmaid   but often
not even a member of
the wedding

Perfect First Draft

just occasionally –
the poem comes out
baked to perfection
& you can't remember
putting it in the oven

Intertextuality

often hard to tell whether
the words from my notebook
are my words   or those of a
more illustrious writer

After Basho

polluted pond –
not a sound
frogs all gone

Surreal

can you open the door   step out   take a holiday
from yourself   beyond the skull   that boiling
self-made cell (or hallucinogenic cave) you're
not dressed up   but surely there's somewhere else
when you've fled the exterminating angel   at a
soiree gone wrong   where you're just another sheep
ruminating on the foie gras   so predictable   this
agatha christie tableau   with the usual well-bred
suspects & the **guilty** one always takes the rap
for the wrongs of others   sorry but nothing is
ever that simple so

> *i guess i must*
>   *be going*

surely a crime   **not** to leave this mediocre poem
to walk away   where the air   filled with itself
plus celestial vocalise & epigram access   just
part of the alfresco deal   your pyrotechnic angst
has left & the shadows disown you

Aperture

harmony is such a rarity   and racing towards it
on a darkling plain   as peace flees
determined to be elsewhere   and you never had
the correct currency to purchase composure
and *if it wasn't for the mist*   we could all
begin to focus

  outside the road   foggy
  like a clarice beckett painting
  headlights   encroaching inquisitors

disequilibrium   a necessity for artists
a mind in its normal state could never create –
the lies of fiction   preferred to real lies
and if you stand in front of wings painted
on a wall   does that make you an angel?
but there were times   staring at the moon
in its glacial benevolence   when you
felt it understood

  the slit of light
  beneath the door –
  somewhere there is radiance

After 'on a darkling plain' – from 'Dover Beach', Matthew Arnold
'if it wasn't for the mist' – from *The Great Gatsby*, Scott Fitzgerald

In Treatment

Some people go too close to the edge and others manage to stay sometimes sad in a safe clearing far from the cliff
— Andrew Solomon

Only when their mind has been exhausted, do the majority of people recognise the degree of Fate
— Rachel Cusk

Holding Pattern

whatever brought me here   where my dreams
don't matter i know you're there
face concealed by the murky glass & those
that were absent   have now returned
regressing to where the dark began
wrapping themselves in reverie   some
seduced by sadness   hollowed out in a
charcoal landscape   yet given succour
by the black dog   *you* have never succumbed
to that willed lassitude   the permission
to lie down   with impunity   as life
rolls over you in subjugating waves &
somewhere you're here   yet when i speak
you never answer & though i'm clutching
some fragile relics   this is a place where
death is free from metaphor
    where all that grief
      & all that fear
        will be about
          nothing

'where all that grief and all that fear will be about nothing' – from *Gilead*, Marilynne Robinson

Scars

too much intensity   is hard to bear
don't admit you've been 'moved to tears'
(or immobilised)   while watching fragile
protagonists   enact a Chekhovian
scenario   or perhaps it's a haunting riff
that wants to linger (Schubert? Schumann?)
music   too sad   to be beautiful   so why fight/write
against that *deep & always hidden wound* & the
realisation   that such a fall into disequilibrium
won't permit a painless return to the surface of life
& from where
             we can never meet
                        anyone else
                                     but ourselves

just an involuntary regression   to the family home
(a stoic monastery   without God) the whingeings
& criticisms (a hen pecking the ground   makes a
large hole)   the imperative to be silent & the
tiptoeing around the edge of the volcano (which
never erupted)   feel the weight of last century
you're still carrying that home on your back &
the strength to repair the past   lessens each year
but grief has its own rewards   when the famous
fiction writer says   *i'm so happy   i've managed
to make you sad*

WWER

So, you've come to see me because you're melancholy, unmotivated, cognitively dissonant. Unable to reach out to all the wonders your world has to offer. We can't have that. As a qualified bungee jumper, I believe in being physically active. It really gets the adrenalin and neurotransmitters moving. Perhaps we can work towards getting you involved in some Extreme Sport. Instead of your current occupation of writing poetry. To my mind, that creative profession displays a completely flawed business model.

Some things impede your healing process. These are the things I want you to avoid: caffeine, slippery elm, fatty foods, bananas, lean cuisine, esoteric acupuncture, homeopathic remedies and talking to other writers. And especially no daydreaming, meditative or hypnagogic states. These could engender an introspective condition, leading to the psychologically unwanted activity of poetry writing. And we don't want that do we?

These days, we no longer want to spend months or years of our busy lives talking out our problems with a professional listener. Now I've just come across a fantastic new treatment modality. It's sure to cure you of your downbeat moods. It may only take a few sessions to work and its clinically proven. Though it's no quick fix. Practitioners in Burkina Faso and Burundi have had some favourable results with their clients.

It's called 'Whistleblowing with Emotional Rewards' (WWER). Very simple to implement, it works like this. You think of something disturbing from your life that still impacts on you. Then you raise your left thumb. That's where I come in. I blow a whistle, causing the traumatic memories to disappear forever. At the end of the session, all the detritus of your life, has flown out of the window to join the pigeons. What a relief, now you don't have such a dreadful past.

After a few sessions of WWER, you'll wonder why you wasted all those years in stress and depression. But I must warn you, the treatment does have side-effects. In some cases, total long-term memory loss. But there's no cause for alarm. At a modest cost of $250 a session you and I will spend the next, say 25 sessions, reconstructing some exciting fresh memories for you. You're going to just love the person you're starting to become! So if it all sounds like a miracle, then it probably is. Just think, never again will you feel so desperate you need to write a poem.

In Treatment

Our interminable conversations must end.
You said things could change. If we 'talk it
out'. Bring it into the open. Where the light
will give it a different colour. The nocturnal
tones, could become a rainbow. Concentrate
on 'the now.' What happened previously, no
longer matters.

Yes, I've been back there, before. Even tried
undoing what had been done. Attempted to
rearrange the palimpsest of lost endeavours.
But they're still there. And this feeling of being
neither ill nor well. The heart a paralysed
metronome. All the old stuff. Waiting for me.
Like a toad in my bed. A spider in my shoe.
Those encounters with the brick wall. The fear
of another end-of-world scenario. The need to
know how much longer I have.

True, I can only smell death when I'm alone. Being
with others, puts me off the scent. So I (perhaps
foolishly) thought, to continue our conversations
could ensure my longevity. Ultimately, though, my
therapeutic goal, was transcendence. A welcome
lift-off. Where being above the action, not only
provides clarity, but it eliminates the ambivalence
of what to wear. But I know you'd be just as happy
if I remained grounded. While I mouth my positive
CBT mantras and stare up at the family tree. Where
crows gargle in the branches.

Obsessive Compulsive

1. Security Magic

Can we ever be safe?   hand hiding keypad
protects your identity & before leaving the house
ensure your birth certificate   passport   credit cards
are in the desk drawer   then use the deadlock
spare key secreted in the hole between the bricks
tap ten times on the spyhole   but return before
you've even gone   touch wood   your home is still
standing   the door was locked   the iron gas & taps
turned off   could this intemperate checking regime
appease the gods of menace

>   *never harm*
>
>   *nor spell*
>
>   *nor charm*

& when at the theatre   fingers crossed   the least
dangerous place to be   is near the exit   if there's
a fire or terrorist attack   you'll be first out on the road
safe as houses & when dining with friends   always
occupy the same seat   for that is where your safety sits
but if you're still on the street after dark   for sure
a vampire will carry you off   & eliminate thirteen
from your calculations   skip past it with confidence
fourteen is much better equipped to fight off threats

but those ritual-mongers   the Aztecs   feared
without human sacrifice   the sun would go
on strike   lose its heat   fall away in a flaccid
heap

at McDonalds   plenty of dining places   but he needs
to establish an arcane order   to avert disaster
stands near the window   meticulously   plants
his fast food along the sill   frozen coke   big mac
choc chip cookies   hotcakes   standing firm   as a
row of judges

2. Footpath Ritual

see the secret smile
on the face of the pacer
as she walks back & forth
back & forth –
   how many more steps
   before her race is complete
   won't count the cost
   so little reward
   such a need to hurry –
   but while she's high
   on movement
   she can't stop
   & worry

an injured umbrella
lies under a chair
in the waiting room

Prosthetic

no matter what you think or say
it doesn't really belong   possesses
none of your DNA   your immune system
or your tendency toward musicophilia
it's not intimate with the fraught history
of how you crawled   chewed   climbed or
viewed your way to here   it's an alien artefact
an irritating add-on   leaves you grieving
for lost wholeness   it can be a nuisance or
a hazard   those corrective lenses for blurring
sight could smash or be misplaced & you're back
in the mist again   hearing aids often reject
the harmony of symphonies & stumbling ahead
maybe the best you can expect from an attached
leg   while the dental plate will simply embarrass

you don't get to keep
  everything
       you started out with

sometimes though bionic bits create heroes
(& villains) oscar pistorius   blading his way down
a winning track (before the 'tragic' accident in the
bathroom) or those braving the world with loud
big-hair wigs after an outbreak of alopecia (or
chemotherapy) & movie technicians who create
battle-ravaged noses   lopped-off hands & scaly
monster heads

those who've lost teeth (new status: *edentate*)
tend to see gaps everywhere   missing fence palings
cracks in the footpath   bookcases where a favourite
volume has been stolen   or mis-shelved   & will eyeball
the talking heads on tv that lack complete dentition

  the tooth could hang on no longer
  quick   insert the prosthetic   an
  unnatural necessity   that conceals
  the thriving emptiness

Cataracts

changing your glasses won't help
without them   you see the moon giving birth
the shopping mall is a psychedelic zone   glare
an annoyance   or predator   *beware the light*
beware the light   further up the street   people
have few features   standing umbrella   a monstrous
spider   traffic lights are scarlet stalks   drunk with
radiance & the fear the ease of reading will become
an out-of-focus memory   **it won't get any better**
without surgery   when almost blind   Lloyd Rees
painted landscapes that ghosted into boundlessness
& belatedly knew the joy of being able to look directly
at the sun   Borges though   hated *the greenish or*
bluish mist where it was never really dark

New Age healers claim   if you look to the future with
joy   they may dissolve   get a second opinion   eat more
kale   a cool boy's name   darling of the naturopaths   but
to no avail   you hate the taste
        the world will still be there
                even if you can't see it

feel the shame   such an old person's thing   **the lens**
will become progressively opaque   but can you learn
to love the added luminosity   *when brightness falls from*
the air   a laser thread streams from the light overhead
glides through your fingers   an alien messenger   so
indistinctness rules   objects & lights with stretching halos
(more saints to go around) & at dusk   trees are velvet
silhouettes   enjoy the effulgence   without having to
believe in God

Specialist

I'm sitting at the X-ray centre. Wait for the results of my ultrasound. I'm reading tortured poems by the sorrowful woman, whose husband left her. From a screen, high on the wall, Judge Judy, who has *been around the ballpark for a long time*, harangues a defendant. The doors slide open. Propelled by the southerly, leaves skitter along the scorching footpath.

Across the road is the unrenovated brick cottage. Still a doctor's surgery. Except for the roof solar panels, it's the same as when I went there as a patient fifty years ago. A thin dapper GP wearing a bow-tie, prescribed valium. For my first-teaching-job-in-the-western-suburbs- far-from-home anxieties.

'It's quite a safe drug' he told me. *'Harmless really.'* But there was an *alternative. 'If you don't want to take it , I can recommend a wonderful specialist. Who works from Chelmsford Private Hospital. He'll put you into a relaxing sleep. When you wake all your fears will have gone.'*

   nearby   a tall cypress
   behaves like landscape
   from an animated film
   lurches from side to side
   unsure of its location
   against the afternoon sky

because of a possible overdose

of novocaine (or was it the homeopathics
i used) prior to the renovation of a
fatally flawed molar   i rang in sick
to my non-virtual poetry group   would that
gum drug also numb my ontological burden
a weighty pile of sticks on my back
on my way   to conflagrate a heart
that's underused?
        the body lets you down
                it betrays you

because of a possible overdose   i design
a space of Restorative Calm & Relief   i'm
bundled-up in a blue blanket-with-sleeves
(as seen on tv) & play Mozart's Ave
Verum Corpus & other chill-out tracks   while
reading Paul Durcan   but develop a yang
perspective   look outward   where
distant planes bisect painterly cumulus &
the bottlebrush (heretically unclipped)
obscures the city skyline   but discourages
greedy stares of neighbours   who challenge
my celibate domain

        because of a possible overdose
                a poem stumbles forth

Recovery

an influenza interval   frenetic life
stalls   time to read at least one
Chekhov story   about *well-fed handsome
people doing nothing all day*   there's
disquiet   though   as a swoosh of blood
lands on the page of your book (recall
Chopin's blood   spotting the piano keys
in the 1945 biopic *Song of Love*)   but my
sanguinary stain   shapes into a dirigible
an airship   that overshadows   *the sad
realisation that everything in this world
comes to an end*   (premonition of the
writer's own death from TB?)   luckily my
text besmircher   aka zeppelin   enlarges
levitates   leaves the house   taking me
with it   as it noses its way   exultantly
transcendent   through mountains of cumulus
denying the tired finitude of human existence

Mental Hospital Movie

after the film *The Secret Scripture*

those blurred corridors
   and the out of tune piano
        just an absence now
               shocked away from her future
electricity rules

& once her thoughts
  were burning furnaces
  now insights are intermittent
       (& her caretakers
             are only sometimes kind)

here   even in summer there is ice
   but she could still walk
       along the shore
             explore its flat anonymity

but would always lose
  if she tested herself
       against the sea

if they give her a book to read
  she writes her life
       into the margins
            an eccentric
attenuated memoir

& she dreams of being alone
   in empty rooms
         she could fill them with herself
(never with those who could not
            know her)

& they could never stop her
    leaving by a different door
       from the one
            she entered
nor would they
   miss her note –

'you have all made a mistake
        it is you who are mad
            not me'

Recipe for Weariness

easy   just go & lie down
I don't have time to be tired
gulp down rescue remedy &
ginseng   burn rosemary & basil
(for memory & creativity) take
tissue salts (for overall exhaustion)
have a strong coffee & play Haydn's
Surprise Symphony & Olivia's 'Get
Physical'   watch *Keystone Cops* &
keep working on your poem about
Side Effects

Side Effects

the pharmacist said – with these you're likely
to feel much worse   before you feel better –
much more debilitating than an illness i don't
have   unless you count a permanent state
of existential flakiness   but those bonus
symptoms   insomnia (the jittery wakefulness
lying in wait for the apocalypse) the night
sweats   (i can't have the flu – it's not winter)
the panic attacks   (you have learned to be
afraid of the intractable child your body
has become) the morning sickness (surely
i'm not pregnant at seventy-one) & don't
forget the mouth dry as concrete with the
taste of poison)   the pharmacist was right
I should be wearing a HAZCHEM sign
there is no consciousness without collision

Bad Medicine

some doctors   don't listen to older patients
neglect a proper diagnosis   give false consolation
even if pain is present   reject thoughts of cellular
subversion   as riot squads of viruses   infections
blood anomalies   rear up in tsunami overkill
& there's no penalty   for prescribing insufficient
doses of chemotherapy   (the patient wasn't going
to get better   anyway)   those spasms in the mouth
(just some nerves behaving badly) & I can't see
any skin pathology   no cancer or canker just an
accumulation of moss   as you roll across the stones
of your days (just rub sorbolene into a burgeoning
malignancy)

> *you're doing fine*
>   *no need*
>   *for any tests*
>   *today*

& discomfort in the oesophagus   or stomach   not
ulceration   just reflux (or panic) take antacids &
valium   all this suffering & strife   pity you don't
have a wife   to soothe away your weariness &
worry (years of stress hormones flooding the
body) & that dizziness & headache   it's nothing
(dead wrong   your patient was buried yesterday)

> *i told you I was ill*

Close to Home

> I let the streets speak to me
> – Bill Cunningham

> What's the good of a home if you are never in it
> – George and Weedon Grossmith

Solastalgia

nothing's like it used to be & here
in this unreal city   unfit for purpose
familiarity has been deleted   they're
selling off everything that can't run
away   homes roads museums & trees
the italian woman on the street   laments
'nothing left   nothing left'
                what shall we ever do

at the cbd   site of the promised yet never-
running-light rail   the 'information' person
with ASK ME on his lolly-pink vest   can't
tell you the way   points to the east   shouts
'try hyde park'   shoppers squeeze through
anorexic paths   once the entrance to fashion
stores & coffee shops   yellow lights   ambivalent
signals flash non-stop   near the cd   where
reliable buses once ran   now an expanse of
muddy ground   stage set for an uneventful play
a tragic tableau   where languid supervisors
in visi-vests & hard hats stand in a waiting-
for-godot-hiatus
        outside myself
                a world
                          no longer
                                  remembered

at the war memorial   they've erected a wall all
sightseeing forbidden & the shadows shapeshift
on the grassy incline   people on phones blur by
speak to nonpresent friends – 'oh it doesn't
matter where we are   as long as we're together'
you could sit down & weep but don't   can't
engage with this place of absence

> *only a heap*
> * of broken images*

'what shall we ever do' and 'only a heap of broken images' – from 'The Waste Land', T.S. Eliot

Disconnect

at my new apartment block (circa 1935)
in the suburb where everything has
happened (& is set to begin again)   there's
only three flats (plus me) & no one watches
TV (reception unavailable in the building)
& Bin Night is an urban mystery '*sorry*'
she says (from behind her chained door)
'*i* **think** *it's Tuesday   then again it could
be Wednesday*' – **& how effective are your
phone & internet connections?**   a tentative
nest of fraying wires   above the unlockable
letterboxes   in the unpopular lobby (fire stairs
are better   no need to meet other tenants)
but just a scisssored gesture from a jaded
prankster   could render you perennially
incommunicado

Impact

disruption comes when it chooses
in spite of your living peacefully &
not arguing with Fate   but on the
hottest afternoon   the power pole
that for months leaned precariously
toward your place of writerly
austerity   finally collapsed (did
its wooden heart crave more
lyricism) your home a disaster
scenario   life dislodged   police &
ambulance arrive   all out on the street
with no shade *no one allowed back
into the building   find somewhere
else to sleep*   ruined food in the fridge
the power pole a termite-riddled
ironbark   now rests on the roof in
a diagonal pose   an uneasy crucifix
this uncanny image   the lure for a
bored neighbourhood   FOMO folk
advance on the block   snap pictures
to entice facebook friends

detritus of the aftermath   tiles sink
into uncut grass   metal pipes strewn
& a long rope curls like a quiescent
snake   you bag it   take it inside now
no chance a passing person will explore
its violent possibilities

on the wall in my room
where the tree hit –
the plaster has cracked
peeled & fallen –
reveals an outstretched figure
who takes a dive
into the pool of unknowing

Flying Footwear

why are those brown boots   slung high
over power lines   hanging outside my
window   is someone dealing drugs &
running roughshod over the street   are
there ghosts near here   or has someone
died   but these are elevated shoes   soft
suspended sculptures   the dangling boot
rotates slowly in the wind   it points
directly at me   do i need to takes mine
off   choose altogether different footwear
see the overview   walk on a higher plane
far from stressed pedestrians & drivers
on the ground

Ventilation

there's something balletic
about a pedestal fan   uplifted
on its slim athletic leg –
the way its generous face
engages with you   before
gliding graciously away
only to return   with subtle breezes
for rooms that refuse to breathe

The Life of Rooms

long-sleeved shirt
draped over upright
ironing board –
person with horns
their back to me

*

chair needs hip replacement
no hospital cover
must be euthanised

*

the cranky insistence
of the unattended
telephone

*

slim-legged acrobat
practicing on the wall –
house spider

*

outside light
makes mysterious shapes
nostalgia of pale flowers
embedded in the plaster

*

pages of exercise book
turn by themselves –
frustrated wings
that cannot fly

Domestic

home as a haven. bolt-hole. leave the world behind.
no longer a stray dog. unwrap layers of the real self.
palimpsest. onion. couch potato. a bit overcooked.
location of creativity. quirky alones. do research.
write novels. symphonies. build collections. too many
possessions. to protect. fill you up. clutter. now seen
as squalor. pathological. home alone. too empty.
site of threat. sharehouse. narratives of grotty terrace
houses. sense of community. sex with improper strangers.
ideas & food stolen. home is the hunter. walking on
eggshells. headache from compromise. a house is not
a home.

home as place of nostalgia. library as a home. art gallery.
museum. this feels like home. says client to psychotherapist.
faux home. surrogate mother. sheep may safely graze.
too expensive to maintain. marriage home. tete-a-tete. &
baby makes three. the kinderarchy. children rule. rosemary's
baby. we need to talk about kevin. tantrums. pester power.
some never leave home. merging generations. tolerance required.

neighbours. acoustic torture. arguments & vibrations. unwanted
tintinnabulations. the best neighbours invisible & inaudible.
renovations. facades in lieu of an inner life. new kitchens. paint
jobs. if you rent   don't complain. no changes. upgrades. *a bird of
passage. my real home is elsewhere.*

old tvs radios. too obese. buy more. update to slimline. anorexic
objects. disappearing fast. but chairs & sofas for lounge lizards
become more corpulent. my bed. rumpled installation. tracy emin
without sex drugs rock 'n' roll.

home as landscape of strangeness. *unheimlich*. zoom in. black umbrella drying in kitchen. vampire bat. shelters mourners at rain-sodden funerals. an ailing heart. broken ribs. dread reveals itself. *its is nothing & nowhere*. icicle a transparent fish. swims down the plughole.

Exercise Class

'failure is not an option' says her T-shirt'
**just thinking about all this energy makes
you tired** 'they called me Calves at school'
jokes the instructor   an American woman
first on the bikes   flirts with the nervous
man near her   tells him where to buy
the best gym shoes **try to forget you
are a poet**   do a solo cardio-walk
around the corridors   **too much activity
makes you dizzy**   don't worry if you are
disabled   this will be good for you   one
woman can't get out of her seat
familiar music pulses & *I'm gonna be
high as a kite by then*   can someone
turn it up   go & hide in the toilet
then the countdown   time to return
– step up step down ball against your
back dumbbells high above your head –
why do birds suddenly appear so nostalgic
Karen Carpenter   so thin   so vulnerable not
like these wellness-bound seniors – arms
pressed against the wall   pull *this* way on
the straps   you need to try a bit harder –

Café Society

Don't feel down   about being upwardly mobile
& there's no need   to ever go home   it's **all day
breakfast & lunch** for alfresco munchers & sippers
with labradoodles sharing the bruschetta   **top gear**
for sudoku & crossword workers & mcmothers
with bugaboos could scare the baristas   **get your
life back**   this is smartphone heaven   *the marketing
manager approached me   though the strategy
may change   is she still running the boutique*
be a health walker   helmeted kids on scooters
privileged cargo   commandeer the footpath
– *gangway   gangway* – ipods   trail from ears
bionic tendrils   **do enjoy the view**

& in the park   where the nuance of trees   grass
& effervescent dogs   **may** make poetry happen
yet doesn't   further down the road   a young man
in a grey hoodie   slides into the job centre

Lost Property Office

on the counter
a fish bowl tilts   precariously
over a misshapen wooden stand –
inside the watery world
a miniature Japanese temple
open for piscatorial pilgrims –
& a single prussian blue fish
darts & dives   confident of its
aqueous ownership
& you turn away   to see
the soulless open-plan office
its garish green workstations
its groups of employees
standing frozen   in diurnal
languidness   look back
& the fish has disappeared
has it leapt out   into the
airy void?
'he's just gone into his house'
explains the young woman
behind the desk   as she searches
for your poetry manuscript

Lunchtime Meditation

sit & listen –
intense thread
a solitary voice
with prescription for peace
black cushion   brass bell
flower in a vase –
the luxury of inertia
get used to stillness
nothing to worry about

on the floor of the sanctuary
blue backpack & joggers
pause in their pilgrimage
rest at the place
where bamboo blinds & sun
create a window
into the numinous

the tread of many feet in socks
walking in circular democracy
on the carpet   invisible marks
narratives of past travels –
the girl who ran away to be safe
the boy who was last in the race
the darkness of late afternoon
the fatigue & sadness of losing
the world   *what is my story   why
do we need to suffer*

outside   city still in chaos
they're digging up the road
potholes   sirens   barricades
hard hats & detours –
PEDESTRIANS   USE THE
OPPOSITE FOOTPATH &
a temporary wall   rises up –
blue mural   men in single file
ascend a mountain of ice

The Bells

It's almost 9 a.m. & you wait for the bus
that's always late   across the road
three plump cypresses guard the church
one   obscures the bell tower   a plaster
Jesus   perches high in an alcove   stone
angel   flutters above the door on the
cracked erupting asphalt   saints pray
& gesticulate   & a homeless man
crosses the street   with his trolley
of everything

it's nine o'clock   will you be in time for
where you want to be   then the bells
chime   overwhelm the morning   give
it meaning   erase the mundane   sounds
of lamentation   yet celebration   is it
only you who can hear
    what we cannot speak about

tintinnabulation   Arvo Part
for whom the bell tolls   pull
harder on the ropes   the
urgency of all that happens
there is hope for everyone

but is it pretentious to want to write
about the ineffable   words disappear
from the page   before they can be seen
still   you keep trying to capture a cloud
& nail it to the wall   then the bus arrives
you wave it down   everything has changed
yet nothing really has   so
    we must pass over in silence

What we cannot speak about, we must past over in silence – from *Tractatus Logico-Philosphicus*, Ludwig Wittgenstein

Atmospherics

a body inside?
bulging kilim
decorates the footpath

*

doing crosswords at cafés
antidote to life's
empty spaces

*

tied to a rose tree
hearing dead poet's words –
well-behaved cavoodles

*

empty room
pregnant curtains –
windspawned

*

fly-by-night
bottlebrush tenants –
lorikeets

*

on the front steps
behind leafless trees
a perpetually musing man

Inner City Blues

returning home where home should be
the howling phantom dog that guards
your place gone to another job   no
friend   no cat   so still the pain remains
that jazz piano on the soundtrack in your
head   *ain't misbehavin'   just me & my radio*
too late to entice some vice that might have
brightened up your life   some illicit thrill
alcohol   drug addiction   frisson of shoplifting
or forgery (instead of moral boredom)
though weeks do fly   when dates with doctors
fill your airspace   returning home   where
home should be   instead the battleground of
your collision with the shadow   this time
when you enter   call a truce   channel Samuel
Beckett   befriend the end   which after all
is just a game

Phone Home

how lonely now are public phone boxes
small message rooms   that lived on footpaths
once   the home of spoken secrets of the suburbs
and Triple 0 crisis calls   for those impelled to share
their human impasse   today no one needs
to be boxed-in   all can ring & text forever on the run

From the Park Bench

baby placed neatly on grass –
the crying & cooing   i-pods
insect-buzz   downhill rant
of car hoons   a plane leaves
but not its disturbance &
at the top of the slippery dip
jubilant squeals   from those
far too young to ever die

Nature Lines

two curious sunflowers
peer over fence –
who's that sneaking
up the driveway

*

sudden afternoon storm
hail descends –
white pills plummeting

*

wind-dance of rain
ghosts (unnoticed)
across the road

*

necklace of curling
swirling leaves –
absent spider's thread

*

in the front yard
flamboyant Christmas bush
wears silver tinsel necklace

*

beneath shivering lights
two plastic reindeer
converse on the lawn

*

on the median strip
broken umbrella –
crow in death throes

    *

along the way
when all else
is colourless –
a surge of pink flowers

Footpath Theatre

Career Change

still sits at the bus stop
but he's changed his tune
no longer hawks *The Big Issue*
now plays a guitar
monotone chords
annihilated by the traffic
will passers by pay
for this raw talent?

Street Cryer

the middle-aged woman
(with an elderly minder)
waits like a scared baby
or a captured cat –
can't bear to wait if
the bus is late?   or just
a primal scream from
some childhood scene?

Strung-Out

walking past the Op Shop
i was almost felled   by
a group of bored guitars
that escaped a table &
landed without rhythm
on the ground

Taken

someone has chosen
the unwanted thriller
you left at the street library –
the decrepit shopping trolley
you abandoned on
a neighbour's Council
Cleanup pile   is
also missing

Still There

exhausted brown bear
abandoned outside
lies on its stomach
over an empty cupboard –
stares into the void

Figures in the Landscape

the landscape is never friendly –
there will always be someone
who lives inside it   see the
naked man in the painting
poised to drop into the expanse
of perilous green water

but there are warmer days
in parks   where a ball
is thrown from each to each
dogs strain impatient on leashes
a child rolls down the slope in an
exhibitionist spiral   an upside down
boy (not hanged)   but safe in a
father's arms   girls cartwheel
the bike with no pedals   runs rampant
down the hill   families in freeze frame
lunch on the grass   the scene creates
a permanent canvas   but the chill
comes all too soon   mothers shake
tartan rugs   families stand   argue
& reluctantly walk to their cars   the
cricket pitch is empty   the café on
the park closes   then the shock
of no shadows

'the naked man' – from 'Head Down', Euan Macleod

Treelined

silhouettes of trees –
tracery of thin
bare branches
an aesthetic
of abandonment
mood motif used
in many movies –
what can we know
of hope & perfection
soon   trees   roofs
power poles   clump
together   fade
to black

*

eucalypts   rusty
in the afternoon light
branches   delicate as
art nouveau painting
thrash in the wind

*

tree branches living outside
enter the house (without
permission)   ornament the
yellow-lit room facing the
street   cinematic reflections
(of an arboreal trespasser)
over the moon-shaped lamp
desk & paintings of Buddha

In Transit

travelling towards the night where
silhouettes rule & everything becomes
indeterminately clear   it's footy practice
on the green green grass of the oval in
the splendour of enhanced light   & never
let the stop sign slow you down because
graffiti never sleeps   but the blue painted
face on the overpass   has suffered a king hit
& remember that *meditation is delicious
but it won't wash the dishes*   (nor pay the
rent)   for the time of the tyrant is now
(so it's *Fahrenheit 451* for copies of *1984*)
now that we've all become *economic units
undeserving of respect*

Sky Poems

If you look high above
you'll see for a while
it's a mackerel sky
no wounding hard edges
packed soft & close
so a philosopher could ride
& write of the way
things deceive & disrupt
why is life on the ground
not gentle & kind?

*

when storm clouds gather
threaten to overwhelm
they don't bring on
an attack of poetic melancholy
just the fear
the hole in the roof
will leak   flood
my creative space

*

outside the window
power lines twitch
tourettic snakes
wriggling towards my room –
& an obese wired-up pumpkin
is outlined against the pole
obscuring my view –
silhouettes of trees
a grounded ethereality
soon swallowed
by the blank imminent night

*

heading west
grieving funeral train –
evening clouds

Reprise

in the front garden
the rose bush
straining to reach
beyond the roof
& if you sat beside it
for years   you'd never
see it grow –
& those flowers
scarlet lovelorn signifiers
sinking to a carpet
of floral detritus
those same roses
featured in a poem
written years ago

always more to be said
about transience

From a Foreign Country

Life is full of islands, islands that all appear to be completely foreign lands in comparison to each other
– Behrouz Boochani

My past is not merely faded or camouflaged under the dust of years. It's not there, and I know a blessing in disguise when I see one.

– Vicki Laveau-Harvie

Memoir

i'm writing in the dark
without a light   while the
coming-of-age movie   narrates
on the screen   it's a déjà vu
landscape   i know the scene
gumtrees overhang the road
like a cathedral   a bushtrack
meanders to some place
of transgression   the nostalgia
of a country town where there
were always too many hours
when nothing begins   this
story is about boys

    but i want to talk about girls

i always followed the risk-taker   Wendy
the wilful one the husky-voiced one   she
went where she wanted   like Angelina Jolie
in *Girl Interrupted*   so normal to be naughty
your mother frowned   'she's a funny one
wish you'd choose nicer friends' but we
rejected her routine churchgoer collection
plates   hymns sung out of tune   cake stalls
cross-stitch samplers hung on the walls –
God Dwells In This House

we lived at the periphery
where it was easy to fall off
though we could never let go
of our delinquent dreamscape

how game i was   then   kissing a boy from
a bodgie gang   in the dark after the school fete
while everyone waited & watched & when
Wendy and me were pursued through paddocks
& drains by a boy we knew   with an Elvis pompadour
high on something wicked & a loaded rifle   even today
could never understand why we were prey   luckily
the bullets never hit   but the fear was left inside

'i am   i am   i am   until i'm not'

Genealogy

how far back do you want to go?   stencilled hands
of ancestors in caves   horned anthropomorphs &
a manta ray ghosts beneath the surface   petroglyphs
don't disappear unless they're vandalised   do we
vandalise our memories?

*

shoebox of reminiscences. kodaks' revelatory layers.
who are these people? are those old ladies in floral
dresses kin? tentative in your cossie on what beach
exploring the textures of sand. defying gravity on your
father's shoulders. longshot outside the red brick
apartment building & the man you had to reject. near
the great hall in cap & gown. mother in fake fur &
turban   channelling Claudette Colbert. you find her diary.
thwarted voyeurism. ripped-out pages (an unrequited
affair). & the romance with your father. *jove i love his
company. he seems somehow different to other boys.*
& that photo in the garden. the looks they gave each
other. pure hollywood.

*

father slaps daughter for wearing nail polish & smoking
on the veranda. she's been wearing shorts on Sunday &
reading *Lady Chatterly's Lover* – while you're under my
roof   you'll do as i say – she opens a door where people
are praying   mother is ropeable – you've ruined the
reverent atmosphere & i know you wagged church to
meet boys under the bridge & your girlfriends   i don't
like **their type**   *they fuck you up your mum & dad*
but try not to judge them   trying to keep you ignorant
of everything because of their own fears

*

when psychotherapy fails   can magic lift the curse of
ineffective parenting?   say if you befriend a god or goddess
dryad or nereid   are kissed by a prince/princess   find the

Grail before the Knights   wear an amulet   learn the password
to a hermetic room where a woman sits at a loom   better
still   write a narrative about the plight of changelings **& why
do i always feel i was adopted**

*

surely the dead feel offended
when they're hunted down by
the living   obsessed with their
origins *sing no sad songs for me*
ancestor stalkers feel **they** own
what went before   take credit
for their forebears & **who do you
think you are?** at quest's end
reunion a poignant void   no hugs
or kisses   recognition/congratulations
no rapprochement/redemption for
prior iniquities   *in the carriages of
the past   you can't go anywhere*

'they fuck you up your mum and dad' – from 'This Be The Verse', Philip Larkin

'in the carriages of the past you can't go anywhere' – Maxim Gorky

A Disappointed Life

Remember my mother's mantra *I feel tired around my heart* An usherette at the art deco cinema. Only allowed to work until she married. Standing for hours. Cultivating varicose veins. As the jaffas rolled. Polite to patrons. But escaped into a Hollywood Goddess. She was the bedroom voice of Claudette Colbert. (No need to ever cook again). The mutton chops and three vegs and her customary date slice for the church jumble sale. (Just call the servant in the pristine white apron). Forget about the cleaning and the dusty rooms. Now she's Bette Davis in a slinky Orry-Kelly gown, mink coat trailing on the ground. As she shouts at everyone in sight. While mum's pressure cooker exploded steam, she could never give voice to her impending volcano.

No, it wasn't her, sitting by the piano-shaped swimming pool, the water a luscious aquamarine. She has morphed into Kay Francis, divine on a divan, starring into the histrionic middle-distance. *The doctor said I should have ten minutes on my back every day.* So she rests on the lounge beneath the window. Where thick curtains obscure the banality of the coalfield town.

Outside their bedroom, untrimmed cypresses create perpetual shadow. She's alone most nights. My father was a Mine Safety Officer, trudging through nocturnal tunnels. On the lookout for conflagrations and cave-ins.

In the winter kitchen, making toast by the fire. But roasting marshmallows at a ski-lodge with Ray Milland, would be better.

Your duty was to the man you chose

And she never attended the Oscars in a backless mermaid frock. But wore her checked woollen suit to the Methodist Church, where the organist pedalled for dear life and murdered *there is a green hill far away*   No cure for **the problem that has no name**.

Why am I so tired?

'Your duty was to the man you chose' – from *Ghosts*, Henrik Ibsen
'The problem that has no name '– from *The Feminine Mystique*, Betty Friedan

Window

after the afternoon
    transcendence
        of church bells
focus now on what was
  normally not noticed –
bouncing clouds   filling
  a too-blue sky   through
        a twisting diagonal
  of branches –
& there were birds
  & the slow kick
        of the ball
            on the oval

never part of a team
  you can walk
        where you please
unlike the neglected child
  who travelled
        to an unasked-for
            destination
in the back seat
  of the rain-stained
        early model Chevrolet
who threw
  her golliwog
        (never again seen)
            out the window

after the afternoon
   chiming of bells
            walk past the man
                     explaining to his phone
'if i didn't have a brother
  if i didn't have a sister
            my life would be'–

his family narrative   lost
  in the therapy
            of movement

Glimpse

*who said you could enter my bedroom
without a passport?* in the mirror
the pale worried face of my mother
as she entered the bathroom   all
those years ago   to stare in judgement
at my immature breasts *so i'm asking
you to leave* i've enough problems
since the volcano i've been sitting on
for years is now extinct   i've finally
lost the energy to explain   why i wasn't
the most popular girl at school   or why
your 'Voyage to Cythera' had to be
delayed indefinitely *only stay* if you can
help me scour the past   for forensic evidence
of the life i was meant to have

Identity

already   it was too late to argue   but
what was glimpsed in the mirror   as she
walked out of the frame   was not what
she wanted (too fey & tentative) hardly
a welcoming hologram   she would have
preferred to be part of an urban myth
(where she assumed the form of a panther
seldom seen or identified)   but being a
human   she was still in motion   with a
penchant for distant places & the desire
to live autonomously (not as an automaton)
in a space where the longevity settings
could be adjusted & she wondered who
had permitted the usurper to enter her house

she could journey to a different destination
where no one else went   but   on arrival
there were others   who also expected to
be alone   could they form a new community –
'The Multitude of Solitudes'

Sprung

my anonymity's not working   the past
has singled me out   sits close at the
movies   near enough for an embrace   or
attack   such proximity   at the washbasin
as I watch my life's lost chapters
flutter down the plughole   it even asks
what time it is   i'm shocked   by the
platitudinous nature   of this encounter
surely it can do better   organise a
reincarnation   of the man with the green
carnation   or (at least) bring back the
popularity of iambics
   the past is the present
     isn't it?

i say   stop this gumshoe behaviour   go back
to where you belong   i've changed   cast off
my strangled syntax   no more longing for the
dystopian sublime   heading down the river of
no return   toward the island of the dead
with riffs from Bernard Herrmann   spooking
the mood   *for the end is not yet*   time for
a reality check   best to hang onto what you
have & learn to tread with reticence   so
you can't possibly injure yourself
   it's the future too

Pedestrians

In another life, we'd met on the road less travelled.
We were children of the revolution, proactive, on
the cutting edge. It could never be said we were
middle-of-the-road people. Then we walked away
from each other. Later, I decided to try and track you
down. Finally, I caught sight of you, striding off
in the opposite direction, on the sunny side of the
street. Could it be possible, we might again walk
on the wild side together? But just as I stepped
off the kerb to reach you, a 4WD knocked me over.

Signpost

after hearing Schubert's *Winterreise*

never much to start with   the inheritance
of scarcity & that paltry space   life on a
short-term lease & the bedsit where
all the furniture had been erased   there
are those who leave & those who must
remain & she digressed in a wandering
absence   straying among cloisters   lost
in a topiary maze   blurring into that
peripheral point   where the world would
never begin

> *what foolish longing*
> *drives me*
> *into the wilderness*

too late to contemplate another journey?
embarkation postponed   or cancelled?   just
a tatter of a shadow left   now voyager
without a pilot or companion & she could
never locate the pocket containing her
ticket to belonging   but even with those
lengthy fades to black   she knew she would
always have music & the sky

'what foolish longing…into the wilderness' – from 'Signpost', Wilhelm Muller

www.ingramcontent.com/pod-product-compliance
Lightning Source LLC
Chambersburg PA
CBHW070917080526
44589CB00013B/1341